Warren Buffett

41 Fascinating Facts about Life & Investing Philosophy

The Lessons From a Legendary Investor

EF EntrepreneurshipFacts.com

Warning-Disclaimer!

The purpose of this book is to educate and entertain. The author or publisher does not guarantee that anyone following the techniques, suggestions, tips, ideas, or strategies will become successful. The author and publisher shall have neither liability or responsibility to anyone with respect to any loss or damage caused or alleged to be caused, directly or indirectly by the information contained in this book.

All information contained within this book has been researched from reputable sources. If any information is found to be false, please contact the publisher, who will be happy to make corrections for future editions.

Follow EntrepreneurshipFacts on social media to stay updated with our free book promotions and increase your knowledge about business and successful people on a daily basis:

Instagram   Facebook   Twitter

Also check out our website for the latest facts and articles about business and entrepreneurship:

www.EntrepreneurshipFacts.com

Table of Contents

Introduction: 6

Fact #1: Buffett's net worth was $53,000 when he was 16 10

Fact #2: His dad forced him to attend college 12

Fact #3: Buffet is a supporter of 'Do what you love' 14

Fact #4: Buffett was rejected at the Harvard Business School 16

Fact #5: Buffett spends 80% of his time reading at the office 18

Fact #6: Buffett has lived in the same house for nearly 60 years 20

Fact #7: Buffett's best investment was his health!! 22

Fact #8: Buffett's worst investment was Berkshire Hathaway 24

Fact #9: Buffett doesn't like technology 27

Fact #10: It cost millions of dollars to eat lunch with Buffett 28

Fact #11: Buffett called on the Government to increase the tax rate on the rich . 30

Fact #12: Buffet co-founded The Giving Pledge 32

Fact #13: Warren Buffett is wealthier than the country with highest GDP per capita in the world 34

Fact #14: Buffet's investing strategy is quite "simple" 36

Fact #15: Buffett sticks to his core competency 38

Fact #16: Invest for the long term 40

Fact #17: 99% of Buffett's wealth was made after his 50th birthday 46

Fact #18: Buffett never attempts to predict the market 48

Fact #19: Buffett's initial investing strategy was the Cigar-butt strategy 50

Fact #20: Buffett writes down his reasons for buying stocks 52

Fact #21: Stocks represent a real business to Buffett 54

Fact #22: Buffett likes to buy stocks at a discount 56

Fact #23: Buffett is extremely patience 59

Fact #24: Buffett avoids investing in commodities 61

Fact #25: Buffett likes to invest in companies with a large economic moat 63

Fact #26: Buffett loves the insurance business 66

Fact #27: Buffett doesn't like dzebt 68

Fact #28: Berkshire has 71 billion dollars in cash 71

Fact #29: Buffett exercises a 'Chilled out' style of management 73

Fact #30: Buffet does not believe in diversification 76

Fact #31: Buffet does not invest in penny stocks 78

Fact #32: Buffet thinks gold is useless 79

Fact #33: Buffett believes that derivatives can be weapons of mass destruction 80

Fact #34: Buffett is disciplined about his investing philosophy 82

Fact #35: Directors at Berkshire get paid only a token fee. 84

Fact #36: Buffett over paid more than $5 billion to acquire Dexter Shoe 86

Fact #37: Berkshire does not pay dividends 88

Fact #38: Buffett likes investing in index funds 91

Fact #39: Buffett does not panic when his stocks fall 92

Fact #40: Buffett believes anyone can be a great investor!! 94

Fact #41: Buffett is losing his magic 96

Bonus- Fun Fact about Berkshire Hathway 99

Conclusion 101

Warren Buffett's famous quotes and advices 103

Introduction:

Quick Facts

Full name: Warren Edward Buffett

Birthday: August 30, 1930

Place of birth: Omaha, Nebraska

Education: Nebraska-Lincoln, Columbia University

Aka: "Wizard of Omaha," "Oracle of Omaha," or the "Sage of Omaha"

Net worth: US $66.8 billion (August 2016)

Warren Edward Buffett is a legendary investor and one of the most respected businessmen in the world. He is the chairman, CEO and largest shareholder of Berkshire Hathaway. Today, Berkshire Hathaway is the holding company for all of Buffett's investments which include diverse businesses such as insurance, private jets, banking, retail, railroad, home furnishings, encyclopedias, manufacturers of vacuum cleaners, jewelry sales, newspaper publishing, and more. Berkshire Hathaway even owns several regional electric and gas utilities.

Buffett was born in 1930 in Omaha, the second of three children. He began toying with business ideas at a very young age, earning money by distributing newspapers, selling chewing gum and other side projects. Buffett is famous for his investing ability, developing his investment philosophy based on the principles of value investing developed by his Professor, Benjamin Graham. Investing in a broad range of of companies and having the patience to hold on to his investments has allowed him to generate a tremendous amount of wealth. Thanks to his financial success, Buffett is also known as the "Wizard of Omaha," the "Oracle of Omaha" or the "Sage of Omaha".

Among other investing legends, Buffett has had the longest track record of beating the market. According to *Business Insider*, Berkshire Hathaway's stock price increased by a mind-blowing 1,000,000% between December 1964 and December 2015. The S&P 500, by comparison, grew "only" 2,300% over the same time period. While the Efficient Market Hypothesis states that in the long term, no investor should be able to beat the market, Buffett has been able to beat the market in a remarkable way.

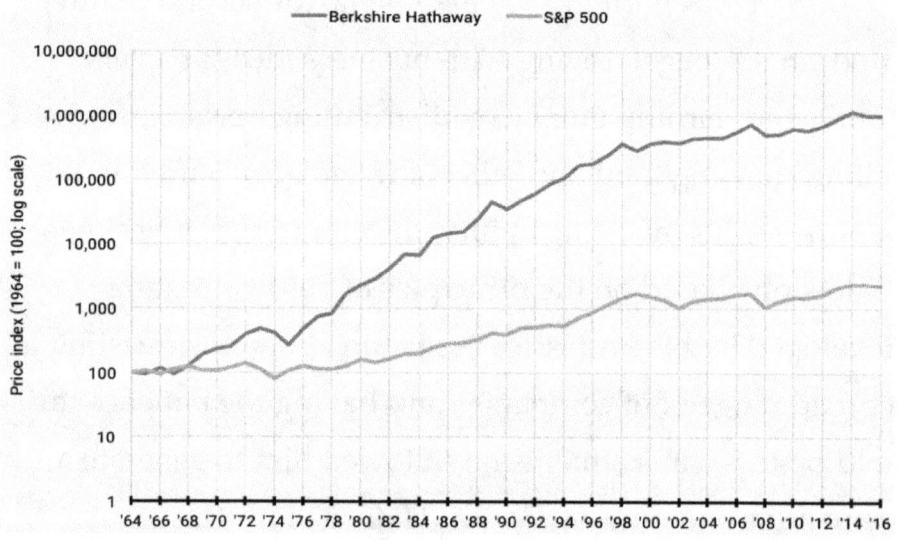

Source: http://www.businessinsider.in/Heres-how-badly-Warren-Buffett-has-beaten-the-market/articleshow/51163300.cms

As a man with a great heart, Buffett has pledged to give away 99% of his wealth to charity. A significant part of this will go to the Bill and Melinda Gates Foundation, run by the software mogul Bill Gates, Microsoft's founder.

Here are 41 fascinating facts about the legendary investor of all time, Warren Buffett:

Fact #1:
Buffett's net worth was $53,000 when he was 16

Buffett bought his first stock at the age of 11. At age 14, he purchased a 40-acre farm with $1,200 of his savings. At the time, he was earning $175 a month – more than his teachers and many adults. Buffett made money from selling chewing gum, Coke bottles, used golf balls, stamps and distributing the Washington Post--which he now owns--door to door. By the age of 16, he had amassed a fortune of $53,000, in today's value.

Lesson - Start early in life

Figure out what you love to do and start early. In fact, Buffett regrets beginning too late in life. Do not wait for things to happen for you, but grab the opportunities that come your way.

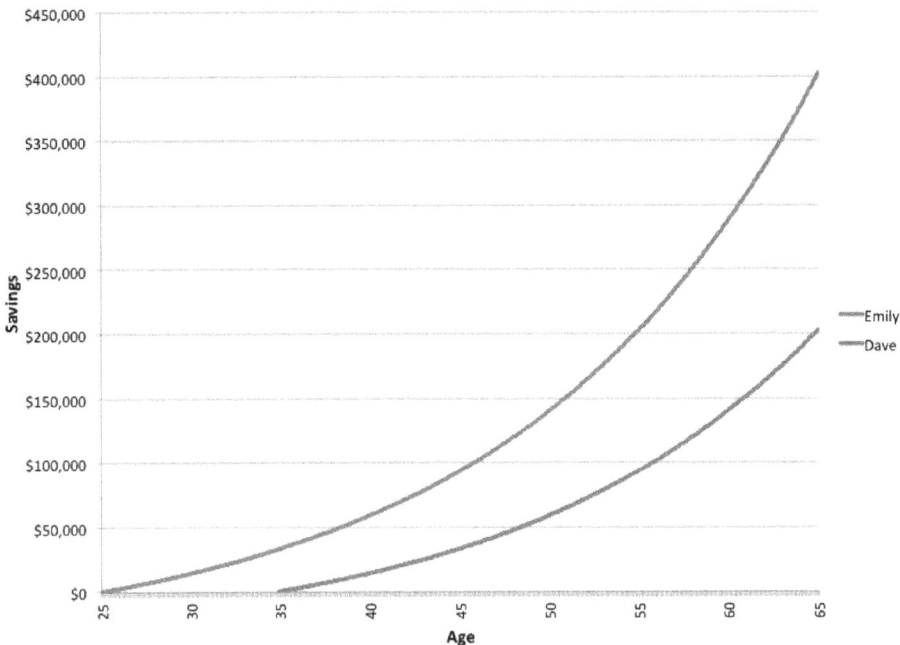

Consider the difference in the accumulated wealth between someone who begins early and someone who starts late. "Saver Emily," represented by the blue line, starts saving the same amount as Dave (the red line) but begins ten years earlier. Ultimately, she contributes around 33% more than Dave over the course of her career but ends up with almost twice as much wealth as he does, simply due to the Power of Compounding (see Fact #17).

Fact #2:

His dad forced him to attend college

Had it not been for his father, Buffett likely would not have gone to college. His early success with his side entrepreneurial ventures at such a young age made him reject his parents' desire for him to go to college because he hardly saw the point of doing so. However, he was ultimately overruled by his father.

Lesson – A good education always comes in handy.

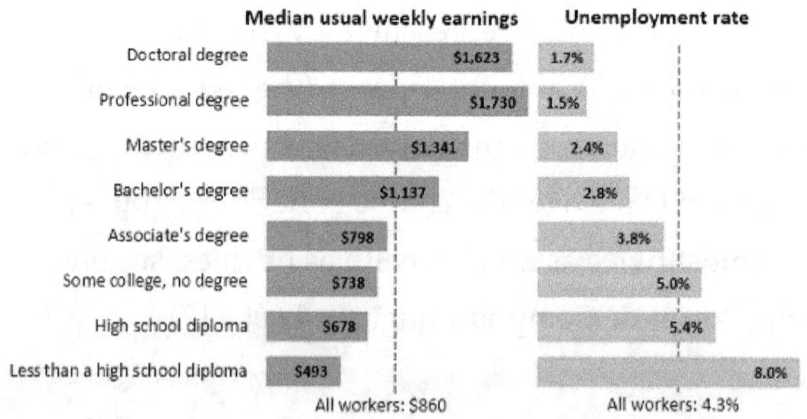

Source: Bureau of Labor Statistics;
http://www.bls.gov/emp/ep_chart_001.htm

As evident in the example above, people with higher educational attainments have higher median earnings and also have a lower rate of unemployment. During an economic crisis, individuals with the least education run the risk of being rendered unemployed. However, going to college is not the only pathway to success. There are also examples like Steve Jobs and Bill Gates who dropped out of college to pursue their passion. The bottom line is to follow your heart. One needs to have a fire in the belly and a drive to succeed.

Fact #3:

Buffett is a supporter of 'Do what you love.'

When asked to give advice to young professionals during an interview Buffett once said, "Never give up searching for the job that you're passionate about. Try to find the job you'd have if you were independently wealthy. Forget about the pay. When you're associating with the people that you love, doing what you love, it doesn't get any better than that."

Lesson – Follow your passion and success will follow you

Most of us look for the high paying jobs, regardless of our interests and passions. It is this approach that leads many of us to living lives that lack meaning or purpose. If only we were to look for work that excited us; if only we could be as excited at 8 AM as we would be at 5 PM. Life would then be a cake walk; work would then become play. Buffett says that he has had a very satisfying life simply because he has been able to organize his life well by doing things that excited him. Furthermore, if you follow your passions, sooner or later, money is likely to follow.

Fact #4:
Buffett was rejected by Harvard Business School

Confident after the interview that he would make it, Buffett told a friend, "Join me at Harvard." Unfortunately, it did not end up that way. He finally settled for Columbia University, which only required a written application and no interview.

Lesson - Never let your failures undermine your resolve

"Success is not final, failure is not fatal: it is the courage to continue that counts." – Sir Winston Churchill, Prime Minister of the United Kingdom during World War II.

Do not get bogged down with failures. Thomas John Watson Sr., the Chairman and CEO of IBM from 1914 – 1956, once remarked that if you want to succeed, double your failure rate. Life is a series of interconnected dots. Each preceding dot is necessary to the dots that follow. In Buffett's case, because he was rejected at Harvard, he went to Columbia. It was there he met his guru Benjamin

Graham, to whose book *The Intelligent Investor* Buffett credits his investing ideas. It turned out to be a great thing for him-- in fact, he might not be the Warren Buffett we know today if he had never met Graham.

Fact #5:
Buffett spends 80% of his time reading at the office

The book that has had the biggest impact on his investing philosophy is *The Intelligent Investor* by Benjamin Graham and David Dodd. In his opinion, it is the best book about investing ever written. Buffett said during one of his interviews that the moment he picked up the book at the age of 19 was the luckiest moment in his life and changed his life forever. Two other books Buffett values are the *Wealth of Nations* by Adam Smith and *Security Analysis* by Graham and David Dodd. David Dodd's copy of the book he wrote, *Security Analysis*, with hundreds of his personal notes inscribed on it, is also a gift Buffett treasures.

Lesson – Nobody can make big money on borrowed knowledge

There is no substitute for reading if you want to be successful in the investing world. When Buffett was asked during one of his interviews for advice on how to get smarter, he held up a stack of paper and said, "Read 500 pages like this every day. That's how knowledge builds up, like compound interest." To add one more Buffett aphorism, "A public-opinion poll is no substitute for thought." These days, most people invest based on suggestions made by financial news channels, reports written by analysts, or rumors. They often forget to discover the reasons why market analysts recommend certain stocks. Instead, they blindly listen to advice, without any understanding.

Fact #6:
Buffett has lived in the same house for nearly 60 years

Despite being one of the richest in the world, Buffett leads a highly frugal life. His salary at Berkshire Hathaway has remained at $100,000 for the last 25 years, in spite of his increased wealth. Buffett doesn't think money equals success. Buffett has often stated, "I measure success by how many people love me. And the best way to be loved is to be lovable."

Furthermore, Buffett continues to live in the same house that he bought in 1958 for $31,500. It is not even the biggest house on that street, though admittedly you need to be a millionaire to be Buffett's neighbor. When asked why he chooses to remain there, he remarked that the house kept him warm in the winter and cool in the summer--and what more could one want from a house? He once bought a second-hand car, simply because he thought that it was a good deal.

Lesson – Money does not equate to happiness

Despite being very rich, Buffett has been able to avoid the trappings of an extravagant life. He loves to take time out to do all the things that ordinary folks would do. For him, the quality of one's life matters more than the money they make. To quote Buffett, "If you get to my age in life and nobody thinks well of you, I don't care how big your bank account is, your life is a disaster."

While material goods may bring momentary happiness, he has learned the necessary truth that money cannot provide a lasting peace. Buffett drives himself around, and unlike most other celebrities, does not have a security escort. He loves to play bridge, which he plays about 12 hours a week, often accompanied by Bill Gates. The two always joke about beating the other one in global wealth rankings. As Buffett has said, "Money to some extent sometimes lets you be in more interesting environments. But it can't change how many people love you or how healthy you are."

Fact #7:

Buffett's best investment was his health

On being questioned about his best investment, he said that the best investment he had ever made was in his health. Warren Buffett is surprisingly fit, even at the age of 86, though was diagnosed with prostate cancer in April 2012, undergoing treatment in September of the same year. Even more surprising, this healthy man thrives on sandwiches and Coke. As per Buffett himself, "If I eat 2,700 calories a day, a quarter of that is Coca-Cola. I drink at least five 12-ounce servings. I do it every day."

Lesson – Do not trade your health for money

An individual needs good health to enjoy all the material wealth that they have worked for. The Dalai Lama has been quoted as saying, "Man surprises me the most. Because he sacrifices his health in order to make money. Then he sacrifices money to recuperate his health. And then he is so anxious about the future that he does not enjoy the present...he lives as if he is never going to die, and then dies having never really lived." Many people compromise their health in order to make it big in the material world. Some neglect personal relationships, often leading to separated and broken families. While they may gain material riches, they are unable to enjoy the pleasures of all the accumulated wealth. However, this is not the case with Buffett. Not only has he led a very healthy life, he has also had a great family life.

Fact #8:

Buffett's worst investment was Berkshire Hathaway

What is the worst investment that Buffett has made? Surprisingly, Buffett claims that his worst investment was investing in Berkshire Hathaway, which is now the holding company for the empire that he has built. Here is the story.

Back in the 60s, Berkshire Hathaway was in the textile business. In 1962, Warren Buffett began buying stock in Berkshire Hathaway, noticing a certain pattern in its share price movements. Acknowledging that the company's financial performance was not going to improve, Buffett made a verbal agreement with Berkshire's CEO to tender his shares at 11 ½ a share. But when the official offer arrived in the mail, the CEO's offer price was stated as 11 3/8.

Very upset with the difference in the price quoted on the official offer, Buffett eventually bought controlling interest in the company just so that he could fire the CEO.

In 2010, Buffett called his investment in Berkshire Hathaway a 200-billion-dollar-mistake. Instead of investing in the dying textile business, he could have invested in the insurance business, which could have produced compounded returns of about 200 billion dollars over the next 45 years.

Lesson – Avoid investing based on price trends or emotions

For a trend to form, the stock would have already run up, which then leaves that much less margin of safety. Furthermore, predictions made by parties that have a vested interest in the stock moving in a particular direction may not come true. Ultimately, this is one of the most common reasons people lose money in the stock markets. The investment in Berkshire Hathaway is the only investment that Buffett has made based on price trends. Buffett has gone on record to state that it is foolish to buy a farm simply because you expect the price of the farm to go up. Instead, he recommends focusing on is the yield that could be obtained by selling products from the farm, rather than selling the farm itself.

On the other hand, one needs a good and a stable perspective to be a successful investor. A good investor must avoid fear and greed so they are not swayed in times of irrational exuberance. In this case, Buffett let his anger and ego get the better of him and ended up making the mistake of his lifetime, which, based on his estimation, cost him billions of dollars.

Fact #9:
Buffett doesn't like technology

Buffett doesn't keep a computer on his desk, and he chooses to use a flip phone rather than a smartphone, though he does have a World Book Encyclopedia on his shelf. In fact, Buffett has evidentially sent only one email in his life--to Jeff Raikes of Microsoft--that ironically became the subject matter of a court case.

Lesson – Do not depend on technology

Undoubtedly, technology is a great enabler. One can do wonderful things using technology, whether in the field of medical sciences, finance, or anything else. However, people are becoming overly dependent on technology, which in many cases isolates them from seeing the beauty of the world around them. Research studies have shown that American teens spend nine hours every day on social networking sites. Contrary to this, Buffett's distance from technology leaves him plenty of time for his hobbies.

Fact #10:

It cost millions of dollars to eat lunch with Buffett

People are so fascinated with Buffett that they spend millions of dollars to eat lunch with him. Every year since 2000, Buffett has been auctioning off a "power lunch" at his charity event for the GLIDE Foundation. In 2015, Beijing-based Dalian Zeus Entertainment Company bid $2,345,678 to win the online auction, still well below the winning bid of $3,456,789 in 2012 which set the record as the most expensive charity item ever sold on eBay. Over the past 15 years, the lunch auction has raised $17.9 million for the GLIDE Foundation, which provides meals, health care, job training, rehabilitation and housing support to the poor and homeless in San Francisco.

Lesson – Use money to benefit others

Buffett is known for his philanthropy. This lunch has been a win-win deal for all the stakeholders. The winners can bring up to seven people with them and together benefit from his wisdom and investment prowess. Buffett appears to enjoy the lunch thoroughly as well. He states,

"Every year, it's an interesting experience for me. I've met a lot of great people in connection with it, made new friends, hired someone, had a lot of good steaks, so I can't complain." The lunch also helps to partially fund the GLIDE Foundation's annual budget of $18 million.

Fact #11:

Buffett called on the Government to increase the tax rate on the rich

Buffett has always taken an unconventional approach, along with being very vocal about his views. In 2013, in response to the inequality debate, he called on the government to increase the tax rate on the wealthy, declaring the startling fact that his secretary paid taxes at a higher rate than he did.

Lesson – Equity and fairness matter, even in investing decisions

Buffett is a man who believes in fairness and equity, which has undoubtedly contributed to his success in life. If you do not care for your employees, it is unlikely your employees will perform their best at work. Consequently, caring for others is in our self-interest. Buffett proposed something that has now come to be known as the Buffett Rule – that no wealthy individual should pay taxes at a rate that is lower than the rate that is paid by the middle class, quantified as 30% by President Obama.

Fact #12:

Buffett helped create The Giving Pledge

Warren Buffett is one of the most influential philanthropists in the world. In 2006, Buffett made a commitment to gradually give more than 99% of his Berkshire Hathaway stock to philanthropic foundations during his lifetime, or at the time of his death. In 2010, Bill Gates and Warren Buffett created "The Giving Pledge," an organization that inspires wealthy individuals to contribute the majority of their wealth to philanthropic causes. As of August of 2010, the first 40 pledges gave away a combined total of more than $125 billion. As of June 2016, $365 billion has been pledged by over 139 wealthy individuals.

Lesson – The highest satisfaction comes from the investments that benefit others

Buffett has more money than he could ever spend. As a man with a big heart, he understands the importance of fixing major problems in the world such as poverty, climate change, the requirement of energy, the AIDS epidemic, and more. He teamed up with Bill Gates through the Gates Foundation, which has been at the forefront of tackling many of these issues in Africa and Asia. Buffett realizes his talent and ability to accumulate massive wealth; therefore, he feels a responsibility to redistribute his wealth and help reduce inequality in the world.

Fact #13:

Warren Buffett is wealthier than the country with highest GDP per capita in the world

Buffett's net worth of $66.8 billion is greater than the GDP of entire countries, such as Luxembourg--and this is after making significant contributions to charitable organizations such as the Bill and Melinda Gates Foundation. As per World Bank data, while Luxembourg has the highest GDP per capita in the world, the economic size of the country was estimated at only about $57 billion in 2015, significantly lesser than Buffett's net worth.

Lesson – Discipline and work ethic pay off

Buffett's ability to become so rich is credited to his disciplined approach to investing, along with his work ethic. As Buffett mentions, "An investor needs to do very few things right as long as he or she avoids big mistakes." Buffett follows two principles in his investing. Firstly, he always invests in companies that have matured and consequently don't need much money for growth. Taking this approach, the company can pay out substantial dividends to its investors. Secondly, Buffett likes to buy great companies at a fair price. To quote Charlie Munger, Berkshire Hathaway's Vice-Chairman, "It's far better to buy a wonderful company at a fair price than a fair company at a wonderful price." Buffett rightly avoided companies with extremely high prices, as there was little room for making money on the investment. Furthermore, many of the companies lacked a valid business model. Buffett is also a voracious reader, which enabled him to discover obscure companies that have ultimately generated a lot of wealth for him.

Fact #14:

Buffet's investing strategy is quite "simple"

Warren Buffett has made it big simply by keeping things simple. To quote Buffett, "It is not necessary to do extraordinary things to get extraordinary results." He has bought into stocks that any layperson can understand, whether that be Coke, Wrigley's or Kraft Foods. In fact, when it comes to investing, he discourages the use of complex modeling. While both Buffett and Charlie Munger, the Vice Chairman of Berkshire Hathaway, undoubtedly run some numbers before investing in a company, Buffett has always maintained that complex modelling will only cause harm. To quote Buffett, "The business schools reward complex behavior more than simple behavior, but simple behavior is more effective."

Lesson –Keep your stock purchases simple

If you can keep things simple by buying the right stocks at a fair but relatively low value, then hold on to these stocks – you can become a successful investor. Buffett has shown that we need not do extraordinary things in order to make it rich.

Fact #15:

Buffett sticks to his core competency

Warren Buffett is known for keeping away from companies that he considers to be beyond his competence level. For instance, during the dot-com bubble, Berkshire Hathaway did not buy into any technology company and therefore managed to stay out of the mayhem. However, as of late, Berkshire invested in IBM and more recently in Apple, though the results have not been exceptionally good. Berkshire Hathaway held an 8.59 percent stake in IBM as of December 2015. Berkshire's annual report showed that the conglomerate had lost $2.6 billion on the investment by the end of 2015. While Buffett has said on record that it might have been a mistake, he has also stated that they judge the performance of an investment only in the long run.

Lesson – Invest in what you know well

Buffett believes that risk comes from not knowing what you are doing. In fact, it is due to this view and due to their thorough research that Buffett has been able to successfully make lumpy bets. During a speech he gave at a college, Buffett was asked how they choose the companies they invest in. He answered that they like to invest in companies that have a very simple business model and are easy to understand. He held up a Coke can and asked, "Who does not know how this company is run?" Buffett once remarked, "I try to buy stock in businesses that are so wonderful that an idiot can run them. Because sooner or later, one will." In fact, many of the companies that Berkshire has invested in are companies with which you and I deal with on a daily basis – Gillette, Washington Post, Wrigley's, and Coke. These businesses are relatively easy to understand. Because of Buffett's attitude in this area, he chose to forego investments in many successful technology companies such as Google and Facebook.

Fact #16:
Invest for the long term

Berkshire Hathaway makes investments only for the long term. In fact, when asked about his holding period, he said, "Our favorite holding period is forever."

Since 1960, the holding period of an average American has reduced from more than eight years to about six months. In contrast, Buffett has continued to hold on to his investments and has even bought additional stocks in many of them. This may very well be one of the main reasons for his success. Buffett states, "No matter how great the talent or efforts, some things just take time. You can't produce a baby in one month by getting nine women pregnant." To quote him once again on this issue, "Only buy something that you'd be perfectly happy to hold if the market shut down for ten years." This view allows them to hold onto their investments even when they are down by as much as 50%.

Most people today think that buy and hold is an old fashioned strategy from a bygone era. Wall Street makes all its money by making people churn their portfolio as much as possible. So can an individual get rich by buying and holding on to one's investments? Meet Stewart Horejsi, an early investor in Berkshire Hathaway and someone who held on to his shares. In 1980, he bought 40 shares of Berkshire Hathaway for $265 each. Then he bought a little more, and a bit more after that. Today, he is worth at least $1.1 billion, according to Bloomberg Billionaires. Eventually, he was able to amass 5,800 Class A shares of Berkshire. In addition, $1,000 invested in Berkshire Hathaway stock in 1964, when Buffett took over the company and shares cost just $19, would be worth about $11.3 million today, based on the closing price as of August 3, 2016.

Lesson – Invest with a long-term perspective

Check out these two contrasting trends.

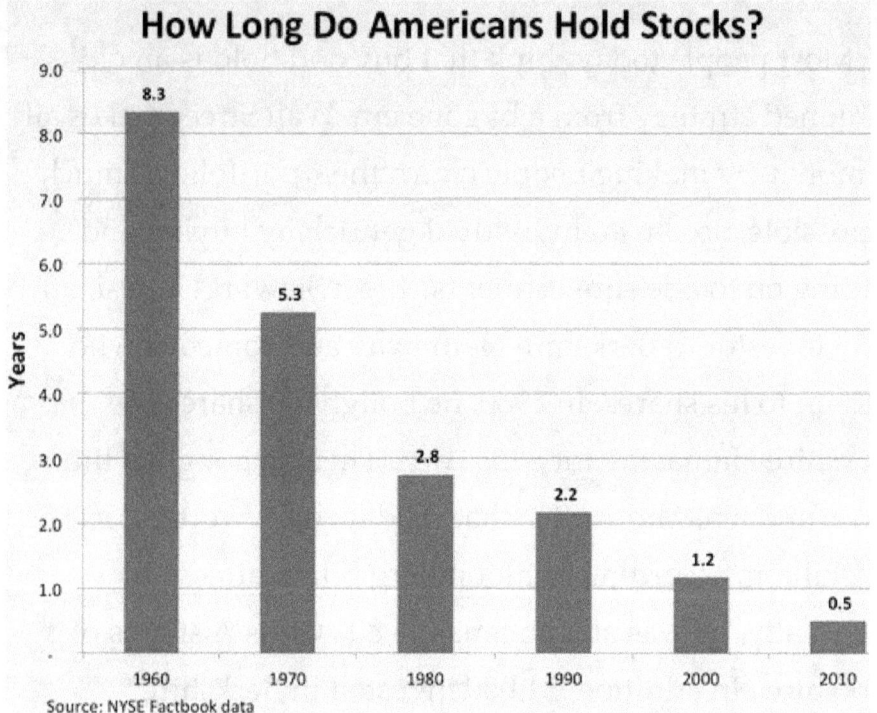

From 1960 to 2010, the average holding period for owners of NYSE-listed stocks shrunk from 8.3 years to a mere six months.

Now, take a look at the chart below. What it demonstrates is how starkly different Buffett's approach differs from the average investor's. Not only has he clung to some of his most famous stock picks, including Coca-Cola and GEICO (which Berkshire now owns outright), but the average holding period across all of Berkshire's common stock investments is an incredible 20 years. In today's market, that's 40 times as long as the typical investor's holding period!

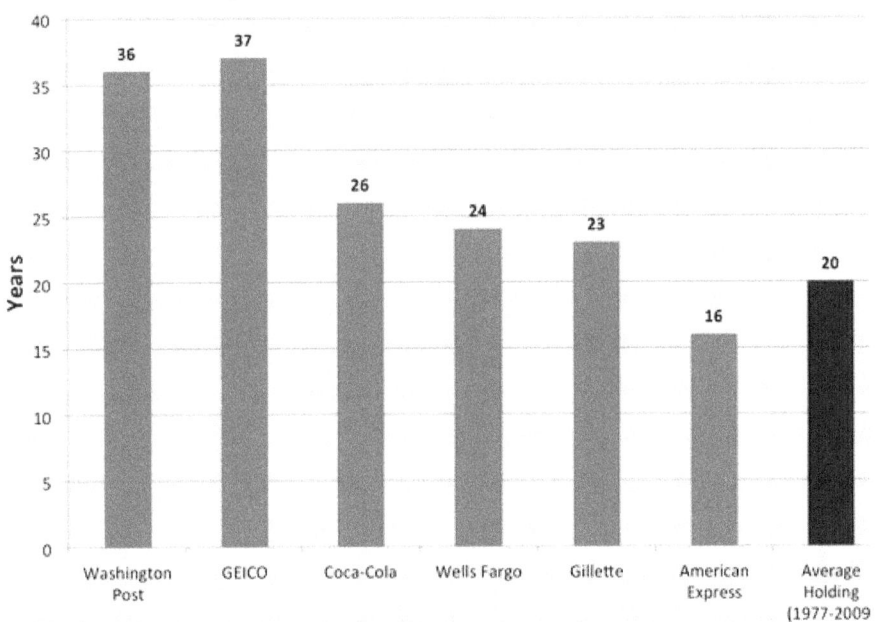

Source: AMI Investment Management, "The Warren Buffett Paradox"

Source: http://www.fool.com/investing/general/2014/08/17/warren-buffetts-staggering-success-rests-on-this-1.aspx

While no businessperson measures the value of his or her business on a daily basis, the ticker on the television makes it possible for the stock investor to assess his or her portfolio every single moment. This gives rise to fear (during bad times) and greed (during good times), which is a concept explained in the cycle of market emotions. As a result, the average investor ends up buying when the cycle has peaked and sells in fear just when the cycle is turning around.

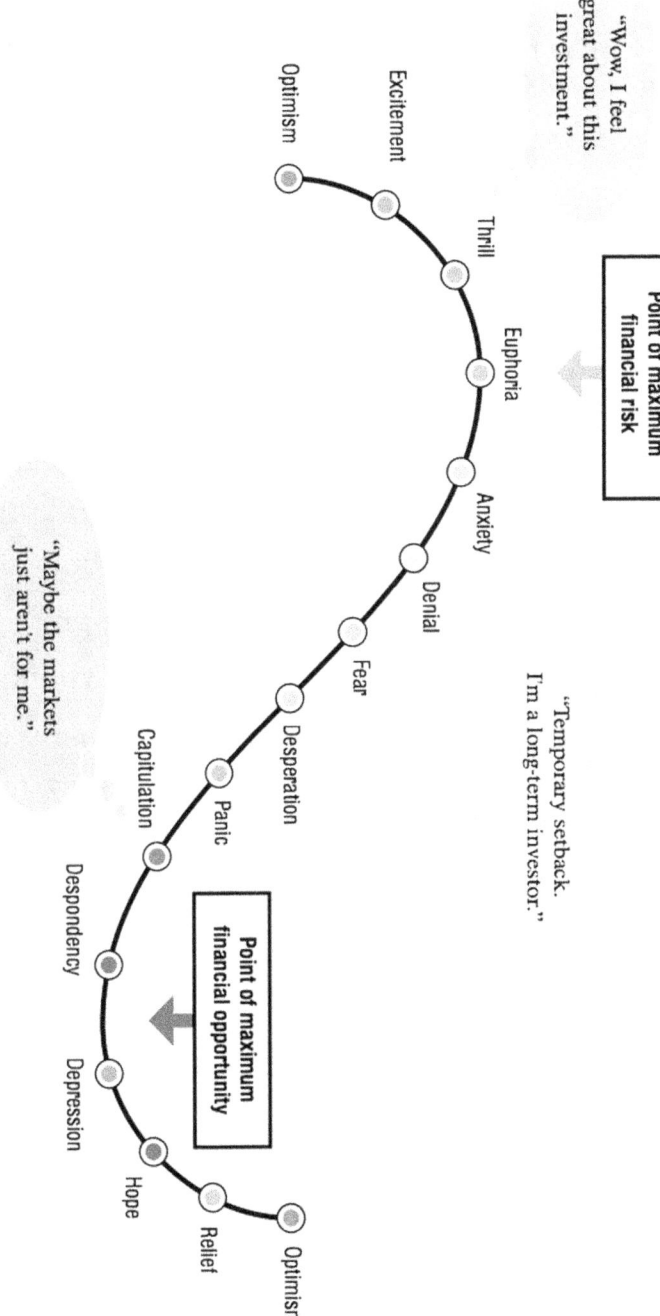

Fact #17:

99% of Buffett's wealth was made after his 50th birthday

Buffett made ninety-nine percent of his wealth after his 50th birthday. In fact, Buffett's net worth was just roughly $375 million when he was 52. This is the beauty of the Power of Compounding. Within a year, his net worth increased to $620 million, and he went on to become a billionaire at the age of 56, all while earning a salary of only $50,000 per year from Berkshire Hathaway. By the time Warren Buffett reached 59, his net worth was an impressive $3.8 billion. In August 2016, his net worth was $66.8 billion, even after gifting millions of Berkshire Hathaway shares to various charities. This means that he has earned over $60 billion *after* his 60th birthday.

Lesson – Money can multiply even while you sleep

Buffett has been able to become very wealthy simply by investing and holding on to his investments, then letting the power of compounding work. Compound interest occurs when the interest that accrues to an amount of money then accrues interest itself. A simpler definition could be explained as the "interest of interest." To understand the power of this simple concept, consider that $10,000 invested at 10% for 10, 20 and 30 years could yield as much as $25,937, $67,275 and $174,494, respectively. See the increasing rate at which your money multiplies as the period increases? This is simply a manifestation of the saying, "Your money works even when you are sleeping."

Fact #18:
Buffett never attempts to predict the market

Warren Buffett never attempts to predict where the market will be next week, next month, or next year. As per Buffett, "A prediction about the direction of the stock market tells you nothing about where stocks are headed, but a whole lot about the person doing the predicting." Rather, Buffett simply calculates the intrinsic value of a stock, then buys the stock at a deep discount to this value (which Ben Graham referred to as the *Margin of Safety*).

Lesson – Stop trying to predict the market

Movements in the stock markets depend on hundreds of variables. These could include monetary policies in the US, Japan or the EU. It could include consumer confidence data, home sales, retail sales, auto sales, terrorist attacks, natural calamities, or a variety of other factors--and it is virtually impossible to take all of these into account. Some people, such as Raj Rajaratnam, founder of the Galleon Group, have tried to procure insider information to guess the trajectory of a stock, only to end up in jail--Rajaratnam was implicated for insider trading in 2011. Buffett portrays this wonderfully, "With enough insider information and a million dollars, you can go broke in a year." Instead of trying to guess where the markets are going to be next year, start reading; find out what business the company is into, learn what the competitive advantage of the business is, and do a SWOT analysis for the business. These will often produce a far better investment decision than trying to predict the movement of the stock.

Fact #19:

Buffett's initial investing strategy was the Cigar-butt strategy

Buffett did not start out with his present strategy of buying valuable businesses at depressed prices. Initially, his approach was referred to as the cigar-butt strategy. To quote Buffett from his letter titled *Berkshire – Past, Present and Future*, "It was like picking up a discarded cigar butt that had one puff remaining in it. Though the stub might be ugly and soggy, the puff would be free." It didn't matter to him what the real worth of the company was--as long as he could buy something at a price that had the potential for profit, he considered it a good investment. Buffett goes on to say, "Once that momentary pleasure was enjoyed, however, no more could be expected." In a letter, he states, "It took Charlie Munger (now the Vice Chairman of Berkshire Hathaway) to break my cigar-butt habits and set the course for building a business that could combine huge size with satisfactory profits." Buffett says that the blueprint Munger gave him was simple: "Forget what you know about buying fair businesses at wonderful prices; instead, buy wonderful businesses at fair prices."

Lesson – Cigar-butt strategy is not quite a sound strategy

First of all, reading [this letter written by Buffett](), it is easy to realize how humble he is. He has been very upfront about the three big mistakes that he made early on in his life. Buffett believes that it is crucial to understand and analyze the underlying business we wish to buy. Poor businesses can often be purchased at depressed prices, but they will never form the base for building an empire like Berkshire is today. While the value of good businesses will keep going up, bad businesses will always decline in value. Therefore, if the purchase price is not significantly below the prevailing price (i.e., with a large Margin of Safety), it could result in significant losses. Businesses such as these also often need repeated dosages of capital that can depress return ratios. All the evidence points to the fact that the cigar-butt strategy is not quite a sound strategy.

Fact #20:

Buffett writes down his reasons for buying stocks

Buffett says that he thinks about a stock for one full year, makes the decision to buy it within a day, then waits his entire lifetime to reap the benefits. However, despite the in-depth research that goes into the stock selection process, he believes that if an individual cannot be convinced about the reasons for buying a stock, it is better to avoid that stock. To quote Buffett, "I never buy anything unless I can list my reasons on a sheet of paper. Before I buy, I should be able to finish in this statement confidently: I'm paying $32 billion today for the Coca Cola Company because_____. If you can't answer that question, you shouldn't buy it. If you can answer that question, and you do it a few times, you'll make a lot of money."

Lesson – Know why you're investing in any given stock

As Buffett advises, if you cannot write down the reasons for buying a stock on a piece of paper, it may not be worth investing in that stock. When investing, ask yourself some very simple questions. What business is the company into? What is the competitive strength of the business? Will this business be in existence say 50 years from now? Can the cash flows be predicted with reasonable ease over an extended period of time? Remember, keep it simple!

Fact #21:
Stocks represent a real business to Buffett

Due to Berkshire Hathaway's current size, it can afford to buy significant stakes in a company. In fact, there are many companies, such as the insurance giant GEICO, which is now wholly held by Berkshire Hathaway. However, even when Berkshire was small in size, Buffett would always buy stocks and exercise the same discretion as any other business owner would.

Buffett says that rather than thinking about a stock as a financial instrument that can be sold at will, stocks should be seen as something that represents a real business. If that is the case, there is no need to observe the price of the stock continuously. As Buffett says, "If a business does well, the stock eventually follows."

Lesson – Look past the stock to the business

As Buffett says, "Buy a business, don't rent stocks." The problem is, investments in the stock market are monitored and valued continuously. More so, financial news channels are often more like reality TV with all its drama. People panic and sell shares with a small drop in the price. Instead, it's important to shift your attitude and adopt a similar view as a business owner--be in it for the long term. Start to see your stocks like the owners of a mom and pop store view their investment: they wouldn't value their business on a regular basis or consider selling the business simply due to a temporary drop in sales.

Many investors are so fixated on the price that they forget that behind the stock, there is a business, there are assets, and more importantly, there are people employed at that corporation. In fact, the whole science of technical investing only relies on following price trends. High-frequency trading, for the purpose of exploiting minor price differences, has often caused acute price volatility. On the other hand, a good investor focuses on the business itself. As various valuation models will tell you, the worth of a stock is nothing more than the discounted value of the future cash flows. Consequently, if the business does well and future cash flows increase, the stock's value will eventually follow.

Fact #22:
Buffett likes to buy stocks at a discount

Most investments made by Berkshire Hathaway were made at a time when the investee company was facing a crisis, including Wrigley's in 2008, Goldman Sachs in 2009, or Bank of America in 2011. As Buffett says, "Whether we're talking about socks or stocks, I like buying quality merchandise when it is marked down." His philosophy aligns perfectly with the concept of Margin of Safety espoused by Graham in his book, *The Intelligent Investor*.

Some might think it's bizarre that Buffett would prefer stock prices to go down before buying. However, his strategy must be working, having a portfolio size of $130 billion and another $70 billion lying in cash. He has often said, "Only those who will be sellers of equities in the near future should be happy at seeing stocks rise. Prospective purchasers should much prefer sinking prices."

At Berkshire, much more importance is given to 'value' than 'price.' To quote Buffett, "For some reason, people take their cues from price, action rather than from value. What doesn't work is when you start doing things that you don't understand or because they worked last week for somebody else. The dumbest reason in the world to buy a stock is because it's going up."

Lesson – Invest when good stocks are low

Buying stocks only when prices go up but not being willing to consider the same stock at a 50% discount is bizarre. Buffett has been successful simply because he bought shares in companies which were fundamentally good businesses, but, due to factors in the external environment, were facing resistance. Buffett says, "Most people get interested in stocks when everyone else is. The time to get interested is when no one else is. You can't buy what is popular and do well." Investors making purchases in an overheated market need to recognize that it may often take an extended period for the value of even an outstanding company to catch up with the price they paid. The best example of this is the NASDAQ Composite, an index of technology companies comprised of some of the best companies in the US. The NASDAQ Composite touched a high of 5,048 on March 10, 2000, during the dot-com boom. It subsequently fell to 1,100 when the bubble burst. It was only after a gap of more than 15 years that the

Index surpassed the previous high (5,073 as on April 24, 2015), although arguably, the composition of the Index had changed from what it was in 2000. Thus, even good companies bought at high prices may not yield good returns. Instead, Buffett says, "Great investment opportunities come around when excellent companies are surrounded by unusual circumstances that cause the stock to be under appraised."

Most investors look at the trajectory of a stock or listen to a self-proclaimed expert on the financial news channels. When an expert predicts that the price of the share is likely to go up, many people buy the share in anticipation of making money in the future. On the contrary, what one should be doing is valuing a business and then comparing the intrinsic value with the price at which the business is available. Additionally, if one is expected to be a net buyer in the company, they should hope for prices to come down, rather than go up.

Fact #23:
Buffett is extremely patient

Buffett has waited for extended periods of time to buy the right company at the right price. Goldman Sachs is an excellent example of this. Buffett was approached by Goldman for a cash injection in 2001 when the dot-com bubble burst. However, away on his yacht, he couldn't be contacted. Due to missing this chance, Buffett had to wait eight long years, until 2009, to finally buy a stake in the company in the aftermath of the subprime crisis. Another example is Bank of America. He bought the first tranche of shares in 2007, then increased his stake in 2011 when the company was facing tough times due to the subprime crisis.

Lesson – Patience is a virtue, especially when it comes to investing

A good investor must have patience. Buffett has always stated that a stock market is a place where the money is transferred from the active to the patient. "The stock market is a no-called-strike game. You don't have to swing at everything – you can wait for your pitch." Investors who are impatient tend to buy companies at a relatively high price, and consequently end up with losses, or at the minimum, a sub-optimal return on their investment.

Fact #24:
Buffett avoids investing in commodities

While there are many investors such as Jim Rogers who have made their money investing in commodities, Buffett does not favor companies engaged in the commodities business. In fact, Buffett has gone as far as to say, "In a commodity business, it's very hard to be smarter than your dumbest competitor."

Lesson – Don't invest in commodities businesses

Buffett has always invested in strong brands, whether it is Coke, Gillette, Wrigley's, Kraft, Goldman Sachs, IBM, Apple, American Express, or Bank of America. He believes that brands help in building strong moats around the company that reduces the competitive strength of other players in the industry. According to this logic, it is unwise to invest in companies in the commodities business for a variety of reasons. First, due to human ingenuity, we are getting better and better in using commodities. For example, cars are more fuel-efficient, allowing us to get more "return" for the same amount of oil than in the past. Recently, one reason for the fall in demand for commodities is because China, a major player, has become more efficient at using commodities. Secondly, commodities are highly volatile, making cash flow more volatile and less predictable. Lastly, there is no differentiating factor in commodities, meaning less potential for premium pricing. For these reasons, corporations spend billions investing in their brands--and it is preferable to be in a business that owns well-known brands.

Fact #25:

Buffett likes to invest in companies with a large economic moat

Buffett likes to invest in companies with a large economic moat, and more specifically, a moat that has crocodiles in it. This moat could take the form a very strong brand (Coke) or intellectual capital (such as Goldman Sachs). In many cases, the moat could take the form of a product or industry that is least susceptible to change. Buffett says, "Our approach is very much profiting from the lack of change rather than from change. With Wrigley's chewing gum, it's the lack of change that appeals to me. I don't think it is going to be hurt by the Internet. That's the kind of business I like."

Likewise, Buffett never invests in startups, because they have yet to prove financial dependability. To quote him, "Buy companies with strong histories of profitability with a dominant business franchise."

Lesson – Identify risk factors and avoid them

In the financial circuits, it is a widely held belief that low risk leads to low return and high risk brings a high return. However, as Buffett has shown, an investor doesn't need to take undue risks to make it big in life. Of course, Buffett has made lumpy bets in companies that many may believe to be risky. However, thoroughly analyzing the investments reduced the risk considerably. Additionally, it isn't necessary to invest at the initial stages of a company to become a wealthy investor. On the contrary, from a risk standpoint, it can be far more risky to invest in start-ups.

One reason Buffett has avoided technology stocks (though he has recently invested in IBM and Apple) is due to the rate of change within these industries. As per Buffett's philosophy, an investor is better off in investing in those companies that are likely to exist 50 or 100 years down the line, and the least susceptible to change. If you consider Buffett's investments in Washington Post (newspapers), GEICO (insurance), Gillette (shaving products), Wrigley's (chewing gum), and Kraft Foods (food), these are all products that are relatively immune to change. Buffett says that what excited him about these stocks was the thought of people using the Gillette razors and the newspapers every morning until eternity. Lately, however, some changes are beginning to challenge this view. For example, with the advent of driverless cars, an insurance business such as GEICO could suffer in a big way.

Fact #26:
Buffett loves the insurance business

Berkshire Hathaway has been able to build this colossal empire primarily by investing in insurance companies. To quote Buffett from his letter titled *Berkshire – Past, Present and Future*, "Early in 1967, I had Berkshire pay $8.6 million to buy National Indemnity Company ("NICO") a small but promising Omaha-based insurer. Insurance was in my sweet spot: I understood and liked the industry." Besides NICO, Berkshire owns many other insurance companies such as General Re (reinsurance) and Applied Underwriters (workers' compensation), among others. Berkshire Hathaway's largest and best-known insurance subsidiary is GEICO. GEICO is the second-biggest personal auto insurer in the United States, collecting billions in premiums each year.

Lesson – Insurance stocks are often a wise investment

It is the insurance business that has allowed Berkshire Hathaway to grow into the giant it is today. Insurance is a business that leads to cash inflows upfront and has associated cash outflows at a distant point in the future. This liquidity gives Buffett the float to invest in various companies. The insurance businesses that Berkshire owns have churned out large amounts of operating profits for the parent company, Berkshire Hathaway. As an investor, one should seek out such businesses where the company can play with its customers' money for years, absolutely free of cost.

Fact #27:
Buffett doesn't like debt

Buffett advises investors against buying shares with borrowed money. In the letter titled *Berkshire – Past, Present and Future,* Buffett states, "Berkshire shares (or any other shares for the same reason) should not be purchased with borrowed money. There have been three times since 1965 when our stock has fallen about 50% from its high point. Someday, something close to this kind of drop will happen again, and no one knows when. Berkshire will almost certainly be a satisfactory holding for investors. But it could well be a disastrous choice for speculators employing leverage."

Finance 101 teaches us that debt within certain acceptable levels is good for a company due to the tax shield. Also, by leveraging a low-cost debt, a company could theoretically increase shareholder returns. However, Buffett is strictly against debt for the company. To quote him, "I do not like debt and do not like to invest in businesses that have too much debt, particularly long-term debt. With long-term debt, increases in interest rates can drastically affect company profits and make future cash flows less predictable. We will reject interesting opportunities rather than over-leverage our balance sheet."

Lesson – Avoid debt

Many founders take on large amounts of debt simply because they are unwilling to dilute equity and control in their companies. While this might be sound during good times, it can be a disaster when the tide turns. With cash flows drying out, the company may be unable to pay off its debts and could end up going bankrupt. Today, in China and India, many companies have an Interest Coverage Ratio (earnings as compared to the interest liability) lower than 1. This implies that those companies' earnings are not enough to pay off the interest. As Buffett says, "It's not debt per se that overwhelms an individual corporation or country. Rather, it is a continuous increase in debt in relation to income that causes trouble."

Stock markets do not move in a linear fashion. There may be extended periods when the markets are depressed. In fact, it took the markets across the world 20 years to regain their pre-Great-Depression levels. The Japanese stock market peaked at close to 40,000 in 1989. Only recently, with the use of unconventional monetary policies by the Prime Minister Shinzo Abe (popularly known as Abenomics), the stock market has reached levels of about 15,000. In fact, in the depth of the financial crisis in 2008, the index had reached lows of about 8,000. Imagine the plight of those who had borrowed money to invest in the stock market in 1989--they surely would have lost a lot. As Buffett says, "Speculation is most dangerous when it looks easiest."

Fact #28:
Berkshire has 71 billion dollars in cash

Many of us have been told that cash is a poor investment that yields nothing. However, Berkshire has always held lots of cash. As at the end of 2015, Berkshire held cash and cash equivalents of $71 billion. To a layperson, this may seem bizarre, but it has undoubtedly served Buffett well.

Lesson – Always have cash in your pocket

In the aftermath of the subprime crisis, Buffett went on record to state that Berkshire will never be a 'too big to fail' entity. He stated, "I have pledged to always run Berkshire with more than ample cash. I will not trade even a night's sleep for the chance of extra profits." Consequently, this cautious and conservative approach can come in handy during times of crisis. At the same time, it gives the flexibility to make large purchases since cash is always available on call. As Buffett claims, "Cash never makes us happy, but it's better to have the money burning a hole in

Berkshire's pocket than resting comfortably in someone else's."

Fact #29:

Buffett exercises a 'Chilled out' style of management

Warren Buffett has a very hands-off style of management. He meets with the managers of his companies only once a year and gives them very broad guidelines under which they are expected to operate. In fact, the Berkshire office is a very unlikely place for a company with a portfolio size of almost $130 billion, employing close to 20 people. Buffett only had to fire a CEO once (the CEO of Benjamin Moore) due to a difference in view on distribution channels and brand strategy.

Lesson – Delegate your work to people that are better than you

Buffett believes that to succeed, individuals must surround themselves with smarter people. "It's better to hang out with people better than you. Pick out associates whose behavior is better than yours, and you'll drift in that direction." Many people are swayed by power and would feel uncomfortable with such an attitude. However, this has been Buffett's consistent mantra. An obvious example is Ajit

Jain, who heads the profit machine of Berkshire--their insurance business-- and is slated to be Buffett's successor. In a Huffington Post article written in 2011, Buffett said although Jain, who has been with Berkshire since 1985, had no plans to usurp Buffett's position anytime soon, that if he did, the Board of Directors would probably put him in there in a minute. He also praised Jain, claiming he had helped make more money for Berkshire than Buffett himself. Humility is the trademark of any great leader!

In Buffett's letter titled Berkshire – *Past, Present and Future,* he writes, "The extraordinary delegation of authority now existing at Berkshire is the ideal antidote to bureaucracy. In an operating sense, Berkshire is not a giant company but rather a collection of large companies. At headquarters, we have never had a committee nor have we ever required our subsidiaries to submit budgets (though many use them as an important internal tool). We don't have a legal office nor departments that other companies take for granted: human relations, public relations, investor relations, strategy, acquisitions, you name it."

Buffett goes on to say, "We do, of course, have an active audit function; no sense being a damned fool. To an unusual degree, however, we trust our managers to run their operations with a keen sense of stewardship. After all, they were doing exactly that before we acquired their businesses. With only occasional exceptions, our trust produces better results than would be achieved by streams of directives, countless reviews, and layers of bureaucracy. Charlie and I try to interact with our managers in a manner consistent with what we would wish for if the positions were reversed."

Fact #30:
Buffett does not believe in diversification

Buffett's views on diversification contrast deeply with those taught in Finance 101. Conventional finance holds that diversification reduces risk, and is therefore desirable. However, Buffett does not think the same way--in fact, at one point in time, one-third of the portfolio of Berkshire Hathaway was comprised of Coke shares.

Lesson – Diversification is good when you don't know what you're doing

Warren Buffett is known to make lumpy bets. While conventional finance believes in spreading eggs across a number of baskets, Buffett believes that while diversification can preserve wealth, concentration builds wealth. As per Buffett, "Diversification is a protection against ignorance. It makes very little sense for those who know what they're doing. Wide diversification is only required when investors do not understand what they are doing." Owing to his practice of buying stocks with a huge Margin of Safety (purchasing shares at a price far below the intrinsic value of the share), he has often been able to avoid significant losses.

Fact #31:

Buffett does not invest in penny stocks

Buffett is strictly against investing in 'penny stocks.' He says, "If you don't feel comfortable owning something for ten years, then don't own it for ten minutes." He then goes on to say, "We will only do with your money what we would do with our own."

Lesson – Penny stocks are not worth it

Many people invest in penny stocks, purely because of the possibility of making significant gains. Unfortunately, many people investing in stocks only look at the possible benefits, completely ignoring the risk they are taking on. Many penny stocks are companies with poor management and a poor financial track record--consequently, it is best to avoid them.

Fact #32:
Buffett thinks gold is useless

Despite the meteoric rise of gold and the possibility of a further increase due to currency debasing (printing of money by central banks), Buffett has clearly avoided gold. So is gold worth considering as an investment?

Lesson – Think twice before you buy gold

In his 2011 shareholders' letter, Buffett called gold an "unproductive asset." He said that assets such as gold "will never produce anything, but are purchased in the buyer's hope that someone else will pay more for them in the future." He went on to say that the owners of assets such as gold "are not inspired by what the asset itself can produce-- it will remain lifeless forever--but by the belief that others will desire it even more avidly in the future." This mindset is akin to speculation. Gold, while used in some industrial applications, has limited utility. Given this, it would be foolish to buy gold in anticipation that its price will go up. Also, considering that gold has no cash flows attached, it is virtually impossible to value.

Fact #33:

Buffett believes that derivatives can be weapons of mass destruction

In the Berkshire Hathaway 2002 Annual Report, Buffett said that he views derivatives as time bombs. He called them 'weapons of mass destruction' within the financial space. Long before the credit crisis of 2008, he claimed that they posed a systemic risk. "Derivatives also create a daisy-chain risk that is akin to the risk run by insurers or reinsurers that lay off much of their business with others. In both cases, huge receivables from many counter-parties tend to build up over time. A participant may see himself as prudent, believing his large credit exposures to be diversified and therefore not dangerous. However, under certain circumstances, an exogenous event that causes the receivable from Company A to go bad will also affect those from Companies B through Z.

Lesson – Avoid derivatives unless if you are not a risk taker

While derivatives offer outsized returns with minimal capital, an amateur investor should stay away from derivatives. Surprisingly, investors often consider only the possible return, not taking into account the risks involved. If derivatives can offer outsized returns, they can also lead to outsized losses. In addition, derivatives require continuous collateral, which can lead to a liquidity crisis. Buffett says the trigger for trouble with derivatives is a disruption in financial markets, which cannot be predicted.

"The problem arises when there is a discontinuity in the market for some reason or another. When the markets closed like the days following 9/11 or in World War I where the market remained closed for four or five months-- anything that disrupts the continuity of the market when you have trillions of dollars of nominal amounts outstanding and no ability to settle up and who knows what happens when the market reopens. That is a very dangerous situation."

Fact #34:

Buffett is disciplined about his investing philosophy

The years 1998 – 2000 were a period when Internet stocks were on fire. Anything that had a *.com* to its name was popular. These were stocks said to belong to the 'new economy,' and there are examples galore. For instance, Books-a-Million (also known as BAM who owns and operates a bookstore chain in the US) saw its stock price soar by over 1,000% in one week in November 1998 simply by announcing an updated website. However, by 2000, the share returned back to its price in November 1998 - a mere $3. InfoSpace, a provider of internet related services, saw its stock soar to $1,305 in March 2000. By April 2001, the stock had crashed to $22. These were companies losing money at a staggering rate. Still, investors were making a beeline for these stocks, simply in the hope that these would be goldmines at some point in the future.

In the midst of all this mania, instead of investing in the dotcom trend, Buffett had the conviction to hold on to his 'old economy' stocks, which buffered him significantly when the bubble crashed.

Lesson – Invest based on convictions you can stand by

In such circumstances, will you have the conviction to stick to your principles? Will you, as an investor, have the confidence to hold on to your stocks, when everything around you is crashing? If you have researched your stock well and are convinced of the long-term potential of the business, there should be no hesitation in doing so. As Buffett often says, one should focus on value and not on price, for price can fluctuate quite quickly and dramatically in either direction.

Fact #35:

Directors at Berkshire get paid only a token fee.

In the letter titled *Berkshire – Past, Present and Future*, Buffett says, "We have an extraordinarily knowledgeable and business-oriented board of directors ready to carry out that promise of partnership. Nobody took the job for the money. In an arrangement almost non-existent elsewhere, our directors are paid only token fees. Instead, they receive their rewards through ownership of Berkshire shares and the satisfaction that comes from being good stewards of an important enterprise. The shares that they and their families own – which, in many cases, are worth very substantial sums – were purchased in the market (rather than materializing through options or grants). In addition, unlike almost all other sizable public companies, we carry no directors' and officers' liability insurance. At Berkshire, directors walk in your shoes."

Lesson – Hire passionate employees

Not every company has as dedicated and committed employees as Berkshire Hathaway. Over the years, this company has proven that when you hire people who are passionate about what they do, and have a stake in the company, the company can thrive. Hiring the right employees can make the difference between an average or failing company and a successful and growing business. This concept is important to keep in mind, both when you are leading a company, and when you are considering investing in a company.

Fact #36:

Buffett over paid more than $5 billion to acquire Dexter Shoe

Berkshire paid $433 million in 1993 to acquire Dexter Shoe. The acquisition was an all-stock deal. As Buffett writes in the letter titled *Berkshire – Past, Present and Future*, "The fact is that I gave Berkshire stock to the sellers of Dexter rather than cash, and the shares I used for the purchase are now (in 2014) worth about $5.7 billion. As a financial disaster, this one deserves a spot in the Guinness Book of World Records."

Lesson – Exercise caution when making an all-stock deal

As Buffett goes on to write in the letter, "Too often, CEOs seem blind to an elementary reality: The intrinsic value of the shares you give in an acquisition must not be greater than the intrinsic value of the business you receive."

He goes on to say, "I've yet to see an investment banker quantify this all-important math when he is presenting a stock-for stock deal to the board of a potential acquirer.

Instead, the banker's focus will be on describing "customary" premiums-to-market-price that are currently being paid for acquisitions – an absolutely asinine way to evaluate the attractiveness of an acquisition – or whether the deal will increase the acquirer's earnings-per-share (which in itself should be far from determinative)."

For reasons outlined above, a company should always be wary of giving its stock in exchange for shares of another company. Issuing fresh equity in this way depresses the earnings per share of the enterprise. This can also apply to Employee Stock Options, which should be used as a tool for employee retention, rather than reducing financial cost.

Fact #37:
Berkshire does not pay dividends

Berkshire Hathaway in its history since the present management took over has never paid a dividend. A dividend was once proposed in the annual meeting of shareholders but an interesting result unfolded. In *Berkshire – Past, Present and Future*, Buffett explains, "That fact was demonstrated in spades at last year's annual meeting (2013), where the shareholders were offered a proxy resolution:

"RESOLVED: Whereas the corporation has more money than it needs and since the owners, unlike Warren, are not multi-billionaires, the board shall consider paying a meaningful annual dividend on the shares.

"The sponsoring shareholder of that resolution never showed up at the meeting, so his motion was never officially proposed. Nevertheless, the proxy votes were tallied, and they were enlightening.

"Not surprisingly, the A shares – owned by relatively few shareholders, each with a substantial economic interest

– voted 'no' on the dividend question by a margin of 89 to 1.

"The remarkable vote was that of our B shareholders. They number in the hundreds of thousands – perhaps even totaling one million – and they voted 660,759,855 'no' and 13,927,026 'yes,' a ratio of about 47 to 1.

"Our directors recommended a 'no' vote, but the company did not otherwise attempt to influence shareholders. Nevertheless, 98% of the shares voting said, in effect, 'Don't send us a dividend but instead reinvest all of the earnings.' To have our fellow owners, both large and small, be so in sync with our managerial philosophy is both remarkable and rewarding."

Lesson – Excellent stocks are worth more than regular dividends

There are two lessons that can be drawn from this fact. First, as a shareholder, one would want a dividend only if you are capable of reinvesting the earnings at a higher rate of return than the company itself. With Berkshire's stellar record in this area, it was no wonder that most shareholders did not want the money. The second lesson from this situation is even more important. With so many examples of unaccountable management, having Berkshire as a partner was likely a refreshing change for the majority of its investors. When investing hard-earned money in stocks, always look for an ethical management team that will treat your money with the same care and caution with which they would treat their own. Only then should an investor start analyzing the financial numbers of the prospective investment.

Fact #38:
Buffett likes investing in index funds

Despite Buffett's record in beating the market over a fairly long period, Buffett's advice to the regular investor is to invest in low-cost index funds. Buffett says, "By periodically investing in an index fund, the know-nothing investors can actually outperform most investment professionals."

Lesson – Consider investing in index funds

Very few investors have been able to outperform the broader market over a long period. Further, since Index funds simply replicate an index, they do not require active fund management. Being passive in nature, they have a very low fund management fee. Over a long period of time, due to the Power of Compounding, this difference in the fund management fee can amount to significant returns for an Index fund vis a vis an actively managed fund. This is the reason why the Vanguard Group, managing low-cost index funds, has about $3.4 trillion under investment today.

Fact #39:

Buffett does not panic when his stocks fall

During the dot-com bubble from 1998 to 2000, Berkshire Hathaway lost a staggering 44% of its value compared to a gain of 32% for the market--yet Buffett still hung on to his stocks.

Lesson – Emotional stability is needed when investing in stocks

Who does Buffett think are the types of people who should not be investing in the stock markets? Buffett claims, "Unless you can watch your stock holding decline by 50% without becoming panic-stricken, you should not be in the stock market."

In the long run, stocks have given a return higher than any other asset class. They are possibly one of the few asset classes that can beat inflation. Therefore, from the standpoint of building inflation-beating wealth, stocks are a great investment. However, stock markets are not like bank deposits. The return is not guaranteed, nor do the stock markets move in a linear fashion. With this in mind, only people who can avoid panic in a downturn and has sufficient liquidity to survive hard times should be investing in the stock markets.

Fact #40:
Buffett believes anyone can be a great investor!

Buffett believes that a regular man or woman on the street can become a great investor. Time and time again, Buffett has stressed that an individual doesn't need to be a math wizard to do all the number crunching. "You don't need to be a rocket scientist. Investing is not a game where the guy with the 160 IQ beats the guy with 130 IQ."

In most fields, someone with a higher IQ is generally better off. In the investing world, the folks on Wall Street, in spite of their high IQs, hadn't been able to avoid the havoc of the 2008 financial crises. In the world of investing, character matters more than IQ. If you can keep greed and fear out, you can become a successful investor. In fact, as Buffett says, be greedy when others are fearful (when the market is down) and be fearful when others are greedy (when the market is up).

There are plenty of examples demonstrating how even highly educated people are not immune to the effects of turbulence and uncertainty in the markets. In the 1990s,

Nick Leeson brought the Barings Bank down, a bank that had financed the English wars against Napoleon--where even the Queen of England had an account. Eventually, it was purchased by ING Group for a token price of 1 Pound Sterling. Later in the 90s, Long Term Capital Management, a company promoted by four Nobel laureates, went bankrupt and had to be bailed out as the federal government to avoid the risk of financial instability.

Lesson – Don't underestimate your power

Remember that anyone has the power to become a great investor. You don't need to go to Columbia, as Buffett did, or another Ivy League institution, to succeed in your investments. To quote Buffett, "Read Ben Graham and Phil Fisher, read annual reports, but don't do equations with Greek letters in them." Beyond technical knowledge, good character is crucial to be a good investor. If you can maintain a sense of mental calm and avoid being swept away with the tide, you can succeed at investing. Only purchases made during a storm will yield flowers when calm is restored.

Fact #41:
Buffett is losing his magic

Has Berkshire Hathaway lost its mojo? Is the Efficient Market Hypothesis catching up with Buffett? According to the website amigobulls.com, Berkshire Hathaway finished 2015 with a fall of 12%. In contrast, the S&P 500 finished the year with a return of -0.73%, which rises to 1.19% when dividend reinvestments are included (Berkshire does not pay any dividends). In other words, Berkshire stock underperformed the market by more than 13 percentage points, quite poor performance. Even over a slightly longer time frame, the Berkshire Hathaway stock has underperformed the market. Although the Berkshire stock returned 61.4% for the period 2011 – 2015, the S&P 500 Growth Index (the index that tracks the performance of large-cap U.S. securities with growth characteristics) has returned 71.4%, an underperformance of 10 percentage points.

It appears that finally the Efficient Market Hypothesis is catching up with Buffett. So what exactly is the hypothesis? Mr. Eugene Fama won the Nobel in Economics in 2013 for the Efficient Market Hypothesis which simply put, claims that over an extended period, returns from actively managed funds will revert to the market average. Consequently, no active fund manager can beat the market. Fama used data from 1982 – 2010 which showed that after factoring in the fees charged by active fund managers, only 3% were able to beat the market. Over its lifetime, Berkshire and Buffett's success would fall into that 3% category. However, it appears that his performance may now be reverting to the market average (technically known as mean reversion). Furthermore, many of his companies with large moats may now be losing their competitive power in the market. Coca-Cola makes 70% of its money by selling sugary drinks, which apparently seem to be losing favor with consumers. IBM is now a shadow of its former self in the computer business, which at one time was its mainstay.

Despite this, Buffett has held on to his stocks, an example that other investors would do well to learn from. If you have a strong sense of conviction about your ideas, you can become a very successful investor. When questioned in an interview about his losing position in IBM, Buffett said he likes the company and thinks that the company should do well, though he did admit that he may be wrong

Lesson – Well, not really a lesson but Buffett is a legend in the stock market

Due to the sheer size of Berkshire Hathaway, performance may not be able to be replicated the same way in the future. We hear it from Buffett himself in *Berkshire – Past, Present and Future*. "The bad news is that Berkshire's long-term gains – measured by percentages, not by dollars – cannot be dramatic and will not come close to those achieved in the past 50 years. The numbers have become too big. I think Berkshire will outperform the average American company, but our advantage, if any, won't be great."

Bonus

Fun Fact about Berkshire Hathway

At the beginning of 2016, Berkshire Hathaway was trading at about 1.3 times its book value. Given this, is Berkshire Hathaway still a sound investment?

Whether Berkshire Hathaway is a good investment depends on your circumstances and style of investment. Buffett believes in holding on to stocks forever. If you are a short-term investor, Berkshire Hathaway may not be a good bet for you, especially given that many of the stocks owned by Berkshire Hathaway have been losing money recently. IBM is among these stocks--after losing significant money for Berkshire Hathaway, the stock does not appear to be recovering.

In spite of its recent losses, Buffett believes that by continually buying back stock, Berkshire could ultimately end with a sizeable stake in the company--although this could take decades. In fact, Buffett has gone on record saying he believes that Berkshire Hathaway would be a good candidate for a buy back if the stock price dips below 1.2 times book value--so a savvy investor could do well if they were willing to wait for the stock price to dip to this level.

Conclusion

Hopefully, you have enjoyed reading this book, and have been able to get something valuable from each of the facts and lessons. As demonstrated throughout the book, if you can maintain the discipline to stick to your investing philosophy and focus on doing a few things well, you can be a very successful investor.

As Buffett says, "Investing is simple, but not easy." Investing requires a lot of discipline and patience. With a disciplined approach, you too can emulate his magic.

Finally, if you enjoyed this book, then I'd like to ask you for a favor, would you be kind enough to leave a review for this book on Amazon? Tell us what you like or dislike and what we can improve. Your feedbacks will be greatly appreciated!

https://www.amazon.com

Also follow EntrepreneurshipFacts on social media to stay updated with our new books and increase your knowledge about business and successful people on a daily basis:

Instagram	Facebook	Twitter

Check out our website for the latest facts and articles about business and entrepreneurship:

www.EntrepreneurshipFacts.com

Warren Buffett's famous quotes and advices

"It takes 20 years to build a reputation and five minutes to ruin it. If you think about that, you'll do things differently."

"I always knew I was going to be rich. I don't think I ever doubted it for a minute."

"Honesty is a very expensive gift. Don't expect it from cheap people."

"In the world of business, the people who are most successful are those who are doing what they love."

"Tell me who your heroes are and I'll tell you who you'll turn out to be."

"The most important investment you can make is in yourself."

"Risk comes from not knowing what you're doing."

"If you get to my age in life and nobody thinks well of you, I don't care how big your bank account is, your life is a disaster."

More books by Entrepreneurship Facts

101 Entrepreneurial Facts About 10 of The Most Successful BILLIONAIRES That Can Inspire You: What you can learn from their successes

101 Fascinating Facts About 10 Of The Most Recognizable Companies In The World

MARK CUBAN - Top 15 Secrets To Success In Life & Business: The Sportsmanship Of Business

Elon Musk - Top 10 Business Lessons Through An Inspiring Life Of A Visionary Entrepreneur:

Richard Branson - Top 13 Secrets To Success in Life & Business: A Virgin Entrepreneur

Steve Jobs - Top 13 Secrets To Success in Life & Business: The Power Of Think Different

www.ingramcontent.com/pod-product-compliance
Lightning Source LLC
Chambersburg PA
CBHW060356190526
45169CB00002B/622